THE CASE OF The Undercooked Burger

Michelle Faulk, PhD

Enslow Publishers, Inc.
40 Industrial Road
Box 398
Berkeley Heights, NJ 07922
USA

http://www.enslow.com

Library of Congress Cataloging-in-Publication Data

Faulk, Michelle.
    The case of the undercooked burger : Annie Biotica solves digestive system disease crimes /
    Michelle Faulk.
      p. cm. — (Body system disease investigations)
    Summary: "Learn about E. coli, the roundworm A. lumbricoides, hepatitis A, C. jejuni, and
    Staphylococcus aureus. Then try to guess the disease in three different cases"— Provided by
    publisher.
    Includes index.
    ISBN 978-0-7660-3947-6
    1. Foodborne diseases—Juvenile literature. 2. Food—Microbiology—Juvenile literature. 3.
    Food poisoning—Juvenile literature. I. Title.
    QR201.F62F38 2013
    616.9'26—dc23   2011037518

Future editions:
Paperback ISBN 978-1-4644-0229-6
ePUB ISBN 978-1-4645-1142-4
PDF ISBN 978-1-4646-1142-1

Printed in China
062012 Leo Paper Group, Heshan City, Guangdong, China

10 9 8 7 6 5 4 3 2 1

To Our Readers: We have done our best to make sure all Internet Addresses in this book
were active and appropriate when we went to press. However, the author and the publisher
have no control over and assume no liability for the material available on those Internet sites
or on other Web sites they may link to. Any comments or suggestions can be sent by e-mail to
comments@enslow.com or to the address on the back cover.

Illustration Credits: CDC, p. 30; CDC/Sheila Mitchell, p. 29 (left); Courtesy Thermo Fisher Scientific, p. 11; Illustrations by Jeff Weigel (www.jeffweigel.com), pp. 1, 3, 5, 9, 13, 15, 19, 21, 25, 27, 30,
31, 33, 37, 38, 41, 47; Navaho/Wikipedia, p. 35; Photo Researchers, Inc.: A. Barry Dowsett, pp. 10,
12 (bottom), Alfred Pasieka, p. 23 (right), BSIP, p. 17, CNRI, pp. 16 (top), 18, Dr. Mark J. Winter, p. 34
(bottom), Garry Watson, p. 21, John Durham, p. 16 (bottom), Ramon Andrade, p. 23 (left), Richard J.
Green, pp. 22, 24, Science Source, p. 28 (left, right), 29 (right), 31, Sinclair Stammers, p. 19; Photos.
com: Jupiterimages, p. 38, Serghei Starus, p. 40; Shutterstock.com: pp. 7, 8, 12 (top), 13, 14, 15, 20,
26, 27, 28 (middle), 32, 33, 34 (top), 36, 39, 41.

Cover Illustration: Illustrations by Jeff Weigel (www.jeffweigel.com)

Contents

My name is **Agent Annie Biotica**. I am a Disease Scene Investigator with the Major Health Crimes Unit. My job is to keep people safe from the troublemaker germs out there. How do I do it? I use logic and the scientific method. I gather clues from health crime scenes. I identify microbe suspects. I gather evidence. If all goes well I get justice for the victims by curing them. Sometimes all doesn't go well. These are some of my stories.

Annie Biotica

The Human Digestive System

Your digestive system takes food apart to give your body energy. Food has to be broken down into pieces tiny enough to float through the blood. The blood delivers these nutrients to the cells.

Part of the digestive system is called the gastrointestinal (GI) tract. This is the path of the GI tract:

Mouth $\rightarrow$ Pharynx (throat) $\rightarrow$ Esophagus $\rightarrow$ Stomach $\rightarrow$ Small intestine $\rightarrow$ Large intestine $\rightarrow$ Anus

In the mouth, the teeth and tongue work together to break food into small pieces. Saliva contains water and chemicals called enzymes that make the food softer. The stomach stores the food while acid turns it into a soupy mixture.

Anything of nutritional value is removed from the food in the small intestine. Water and salt is removed in the large intestine. Also in the large intestine are lots of "good" bacteria called normal flora. These bacteria help us in a lot of ways. They fight off bad bacteria. They even make our vitamins B and K.

When everything of nutritional value has been removed, feces, or stool, is left. The stool is pushed out of the body through the anus. Feces can contain lots of live normal flora bacteria. While these bacteria help us in the large intestine, in the upper GI tract they cause serious diseases. This happens when food or water is contaminated with feces.

An infection occurs if live bacteria multiply inside a victim and cause disease. When bacteria inside a victim release poisonous toxins it is called an intoxication. When GI tracts are attacked by microbes people often suffer from dehydration. This occurs when the body doesn't get enough water.

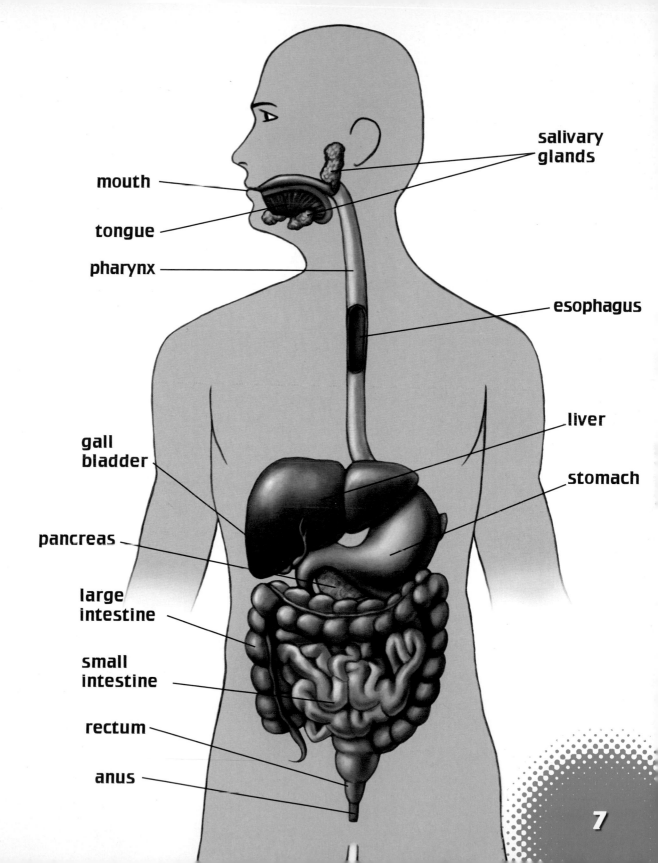

salivary
glands

mouth

tongue

pharynx

esophagus

liver

gall
bladder

stomach

pancreas

large
intestine

small
intestine

rectum

anus

7

THE CASE OF
the *Undercooked Burger*

The Crime

Eleven-year-old Manny and his family went to the beach for summer vacation. On their first night they grilled hamburgers. As Manny's mother mixed the meat and bread crumbs he watched over his four-year-old sister Abelena. Everyone enjoyed dinner because the burgers were juicy and delicious. Unfortunately, the beach vacation came to a grinding halt several days later when everyone got sick.

The Clues

I met Manny and his family at the hospital three days into their vacation. These were their symptoms:

 Severe stomach cramps

Bloody diarrhea

Manny and his sister had minor fevers

The Suspect

The family's symptoms all pointed toward a digestive system attack. The suspects could be bacterial, viral, or fungal. I questioned the family on everything they had eaten in the last five days. When I heard about hamburgers cooked rare I had my suspect. To a health crimes investigator, ground beef and the symptom of bloody diarrhea means *Escherichia coli* O157:H7.

This bad guy has been on the major health crimes most wanted list for years. Many members of the *E. coli* family are law-abiding bacteria, but *E. coli* O157:H7 has gone over to the dark side.

DISEASE REPEAT OFFENDERS

Once inside the body this violent microbe clings to our cells and invades our tissues. It then makes a toxin that kills our cells. All of this destruction causes the trademark symptom of bloody diarrhea.

E. coli O157:H7 can enter victims in unpasteurized milk and raw vegetables. It often hitches a ride in ground beef. Cows do not become sick like people so no one knows O157:H7 is hiding in them. Contaminated ground beef must be cooked thoroughly to kill the E. coli. If not, serious disease occurs. Some doctors believe it only takes ten bacteria to make you sick.

SUSPECT: E. coli O157:H7

Test One — Test the Family for *E. coli* O157:H7

I took stool samples from Manny's family. I spread each sample on an agar plate. I knew the samples would contain many normal bacteria so I used a special agar. Sorbital MacConkey Agar contains the sugar sorbitol. When O157:H7 munch on sorbitol they produce acids. Chemicals in the agar will show O157:H7 as colorless and other bacteria as pink.

Result: Colorless bacteria were present on all four agar plates.

Colorless colonies of *E. coli* O157:H7 grew on the agar for all members of the family.

The Polymerase Chain Reaction (PCR) Test

I took the colorless bacteria from the Test One agar plates. I then performed the PCR test to see if these bacteria were really *E. coli* O157:H7. The PCR test looks for the DNA inside the *E. coli*. PCR is very specific and sensitive.

Result: *E. coli* O157:H7 was positively identified inside each family member.

The polymerase chain reaction test was positive.

The Verdict

E. coli O157:H7 was found guilty on all counts of attacking Manny's family.

CONVICTED GERM: *E. coli*

Justice

E. coli O157:H7 poisoning is a very difficult disease to cure. Medicines that stop diarrhea can help O157:H7 stay inside the victim. They also increase the risk of dehydration. Antibiotics do not seem to help. All we could do was watch over Manny's family while their immune systems fought the O157:H7.

Manny and his parents recovered from their attacks. Abelena became sicker. Seven days after her symptoms first appeared she was weak and had trouble urinating. Abelena had developed hemolytic uremic syndrome (HUS).

About 5 to 10 percent of young children attacked by *E. coli* O157:H7 develop HUS. This happens when the O157:H7 toxin convinces the immune system to flood the body with chemicals. These chemicals help fight invaders. But releasing too many of these chemicals at once damages the kidneys. A kidney transplant saved Abelena's life.

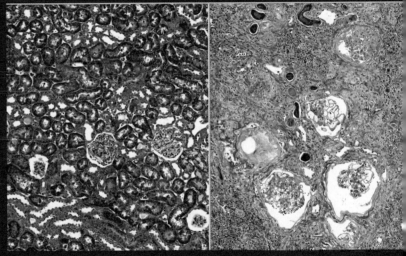

On the left is the tissue of a healthy kidney. On the right is the tissue of Abelena's kidney. The blue color shows the damaged areas.

This is Agent Annie Biotica signing off. Stay safe out there.

Chapter 2

THE CASE OF
the Stowaway Worm

The Crime

Thirteen-year-old Vidisha visited her grandmother for three months in Louisiana. She loved the food! When she returned home her mother commented on how Vidisha had gained a cute little potbelly. Unfortunately, that cute pot belly turned out to be a health crime.

A few weeks after being home Vidisha was taken to the doctor. These were her symptoms:

 Abdominal pains

Fever

Diarrhea

This seemed like a misdemeanor stomach virus attack. Her doctor sent her home. Two weeks later Vidisha was worse. Now she couldn't go to the bathroom at all. I met Vidisha and her family at the ER.

As I was examining Vidisha she began to vomit. I quickly handed her a plastic bowl. When she was done I left the room with the bowl. I didn't want Vidisha to see the large white worm she had thrown up.

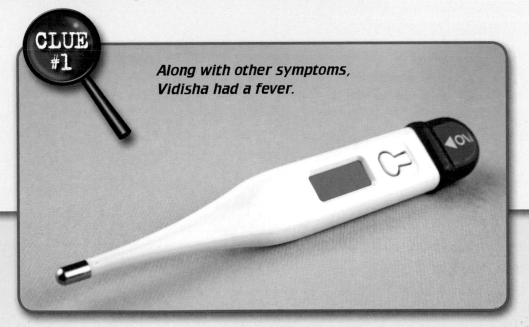

CLUE #1

Along with other symptoms, Vidisha had a fever.

I matched the captured worm to mugshot photos and identified it as *Ascaris lumbricoides.* This is a type of roundworm and it is responsible for most of the worm infections in the world.

SUSPECT: *Ascaris lumbricoides*

The life cycle of this slimy criminal begins when worms inside a person lay eggs. The eggs exit the body in the feces. If people are not careful about cleanliness, feces can contaminate water and food. This is how a new victim swallows the worm eggs.

Once inside a new victim the *A. lumbricoides* eggs hatch into larvae. Larvae look like tiny worms. The larvae tunnel through the intestinal wall into the bloodstream. They travel the bloodstream to the lungs. They hide here for a few weeks and grow bigger. To complete their life cycle they need to return to the intestines. To do this, the larvae make the victim cough. The coughing shoots the larvae up into the throat where they are swallowed. In the intestines the worms survive off the food the victim eats and can grow to be twelve inches long. While they are there they constantly release eggs.

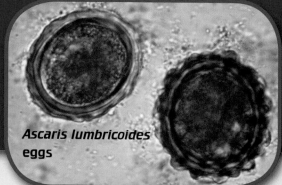

Ascaris lumbricoides eggs

The Evidence

I knew the identity of Vidisha's attacker. Now I needed to determine the seriousness of Vidisha's worm infestation.

Test One X-Rays of Vidisha's Abdomen

A special type of photographic film was placed behind Vidisha's body. X-rays are beams of energy. A machine sent the X-rays toward her body. The X-rays can pass through only some parts of the body. A picture on the photographic film was created that showed what was inside Vidisha's body.

Result: Vidisha's X-ray showed a large number of worms in her small intestines. The X-ray also showed the worms to be tangled into a knotted mess.

A large number of tangled worms (pink) were in Vidisha's intestines.

The Verdict

Based on Vidisha's X-ray and the worm she vomited up, *A. lumbricoides* was found guilty on all counts of this digestive system attack. It was time to kick these trespassers out!

CONVICTED: Ascaris lumbricoides

Justice

Vidisha had so many worms in her that she was in grave danger. The worms inside Vidisha had caused an obstruction. This meant they had completely blocked her intestines. The doctors gave Vidisha medicine that would make the worms slippery. Unfortunately, there were too many and they were stuck tight.

Vidisha was so dehydrated that her life was in danger. A surgeon was called in. She did not cut into the intestines. The normal bacteria could get loose and cause disease in other parts of the body. Instead, she gently kneaded Vidisha's intestine with her fingers to untangle the knot of worms. She then "milked" the worms down into the large intestine. After three days Vidisha's body pushed out most of the worms. Before she went home Vidisha was given medicine to kill any remaining worms.

Ascaris lumbricoides *worms were removed from Vidisha.*

This is Agent Annie Biotica signing off. Stay safe out there.

Chapter 3

THE CASE OF
the Deadly Onions

The Crime

The Perez family was celebrating Grandma's eighty-fifth birthday. They had a party at their favorite restaurant. Almost two weeks later the Perez family was no longer celebrating. Grandma was so sick and was taken to the hospital. That's when I got the call.

When I arrived at the hospital these were Grandma's symptoms:

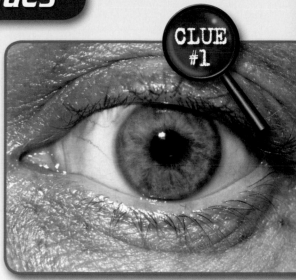

- Dark urine (the color of cola)
- Yellowish (jaundiced) skin and whites of the eyes
- Nausea
- Vomiting
- Low fever
- Body aches
- Abdominal pains

Grandma Perez's skin and the whites of her eyes were yellow.

The Suspect

The dark urine and jaundice stood out as important clues. They told me Grandma's liver had been attacked. When the liver is damaged it releases a yellow-brown substance. The substance collects in the skin and the whites of the eyes, turning them yellow. As it exits the body it makes the urine dark brown.

For a liver attack I immediately suspected a hepatitis virus. This viral crime family is divided into seven gangs called hepatitis A, B, C, D, E, F, and G. I was considering which gang might have committed this crime when Grandma's daughter Juanita vomited. The whites of her eyes were jaundiced. Grandma's was not an isolated attack.

Family member	Symptoms	Date symptoms began
Grandma	Yes	Five days ago—October 18th
Juanita	Yes	October 20th
Two of Juanita's daughters (ages 32 & 40)	Yes	October 20th
Juanita's husband	No	
Juanita's grandchildren (oldest age 7)	No	

I examined the entire family and this is what I found out:

Four people in the family were hit. The fact that their symptoms began within days of each other suggested that they had been attacked at the same time. All the victims had eaten together at the party. This narrowed my suspect list to hepatitis A virus (HAV) because it attacks through food.

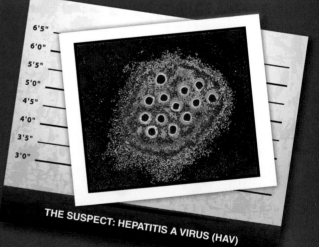

THE SUSPECT: HEPATITIS A VIRUS (HAV)

The Case of the Undercooked Burger

The Evidence

Test One: Test The Perez Family's Blood for Anti-HAV Antibodies

When someone is attacked by HAV his immune system makes proteins called antibodies. These grab and hold onto attackers until the body can eliminate them. The immune system makes different antibodies. People with a current HAV infection will have IgM antibodies in their blood. HAV survivors will have IgG antibodies. IgG protects against future attacks.

The IgM (left) and IgG (right) antibodies

Juanita's husband must have already survived an HAV attack. All the grandchildren had been vaccinated against HAV. They should all have IgG antibodies.

Results of the blood tests:

Family member	Type of HAV Antibody	Currently Under Attack
Grandma	IgM	Yes
Juanita	IgM	Yes
Two of Juanita's daughters	IgM	Yes
Juanita's husband	IgG	No
Juanita's grandchildren	IgG	No

Because Grandma, Juanita, and Juanita's two daughters did not have protective IgG antibodies, they had been attacked by HAV.

The Verdict

The hepatitis A virus was found guilty on all counts of attacking members of the Perez family.

CONVICTED GERM
Hepatitis A virus

Justice

There is no cure for an HAV infection. In most people this attack is not serious and the immune system fights off the virus in a few months. Since Grandma was older she stayed in the hospital and got lots of fluids. The Perez victims eventually recovered.

Because this attack occurred in a public restaurant I knew there may have been more victims. I checked the health crimes database. From October 1st to the 8th, 578 people in the city had been attacked by HAV. Each victim had eaten at that restaurant. Each victim's meal contained green onions.

I reported the farm that grew the green onions to the United States Food and Drug Administration (FDA). After an investigation, the FDA linked onions from that farm to HAV outbreaks in three other states. How the onions became contaminated with HAV remains a mystery.

This is Agent Annie Biotica signing off. Stay safe out there.

Chapter (4)

THE CASE OF
the *Chicken Juice* and
the *Cutting Board*

The Crime

The Mancini family had a family reunion picnic. There were all kinds of homemade foods. Uncle Mario even made his famous barbecued chicken. After cutting up fresh whole chickens he grilled them in his secret recipe barbecue sauce.
It was a wonderful reunion, but five days later three young girls were in the hospital.

The Clues

I met the victims at the hospital. They were sisters, ages 16, 14, and 12. These were their symptoms:

   Bloody diarrhea

- Abdominal cramps
- Vomiting
- Fever
- Headache
- Muscle pains

Vomiting and diarrhea indicate a violent digestive system attack. I needed to know what these girls had eaten recently. I learned from their frustrated mother that for weeks the girls had only been eating celery. After they read that their favorite pop singer only eats celery to stay thin, they were not interested in eating anything else. However, their mother had insisted the girls eat at the reunion. She remembered how they had angrily stomped off with their plates of Uncle Mario's chicken to eat by themselves.

The three sisters were experiencing a digestive system attack.

Raw chicken prepared at a picnic is often a recipe for food poisoning. The bacterial offender *Salmonella* often hides in raw chicken. The symptoms of a *Salmonella* attack match what the girls were experiencing. What did not fit was that many other people ate Uncle Mario's chicken and did not get sick. I continued to question the girls. Eventually the youngest sister spilled the beans. They had never eaten the chicken. They had thrown it away. Then they had searched through coolers until they found celery. They then used Uncle Mario's cutting board to slice celery sticks small enough to hide in their pockets. That cutting board had been covered in raw chicken juice! Now I had another suspect. *Campylobacter jejuni*, who also hides in raw chicken juice. Because fewer than five hundred bacteria can cause serious illness, *C. jejuni* are the number one cause of diarrheal attacks in the United States.

SUSPECT #1: SALMONELLA

The bacterial offender Salmonella often hides in raw chicken.

The girls had used a cutting board covered in raw chicken juice.

SUSPECT #2 : CAMPYLOBACTER JEJUNI

✓ The Evidence

Test One — Which Bacteria Is Inside the Girls?

I took a stool sample from each girl and put the samples on two different types of agar. Because *C. jejuni* are very uncooperative in the laboratory I used special agar plates containing their favorite foods. This agar also contains antibiotics to prevent other bacteria from growing. The other agar is made to identify *Salmonella*. They will appear yellow. Other bacteria will be different colors or won't grow at all.

Result: *C. jejuni* grew from each girl's sample. No *Salmonella* grew. This was strong evidence against *Campylobacter jejuni*. But two positive IDs are always better than one.

C. jejuni

✓ The test plates (above) for each girl grew *C. jejuni*. *Salmonella* (right) was eliminated as a suspct in this crime.

Test Two

The Gram Stain

I took samples of the bacteria from the agar plates. I spread each sample on a glass microscope slide and performed the Gram stain. Under the microscope *C. jejuni* will appear pink (gram-negative) and spiral shaped.

Result: In each sample I saw curvy pink rods.

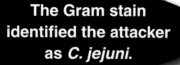

The Gram stain identified the attacker as *C. jejuni*.

The Verdict

Campylobacter jejuni was found guilty on all counts of attacking the three sisters.

Justice

A healthy immune system will eventually evict *C. jejuni* trespassers. However, these girls were very thin and malnourished because of their dangerous celery diet. Because I feared that their immune systems had been weakened by the diet, I gave them antibiotics. I also kept the sisters in the hospital. They got plenty of fluids to prevent dehydration. They had no choice but to eat nutritious meals. After a week the girls went home healthy and with a new attitude about eating properly.

This is Agent Annie Biotica signing off. Stay safe out there.

Chapter 5

THE CASE OF
the Poisoned Chili

The Crime

Charles Peters was eighty-five years old and ived by himself. On a cold winter day he decided to make some chili. It was so good that he had it for dinner the next three nights. The only problem was that he got very ill that third night. Charles called a neighbor to take him to the hospital.

The Clues

When I met Charles at the hospital this is what I found out:

 He had finished eating dinner at 5:30 P.M. He went to bed at 10:00 P.M. At 11:30 P.M. he woke up feeling nauseous and was soon vomiting.

Horribly painful abdominal cramps began as he continued to vomit.

Then the diarrhea began.

The Suspect

There are many microbe villains that cause these digestive crime symptoms. Logically, I began by asking Charles what he had eaten recently. I found out he had eaten the same batch of chili three days in a row. I began to wonder if a microbe had invaded and grown in the chili. This could have happened if his refrigerator was not cold enough. When I asked Charles about his refrigerator he seemed embarrassed. He told me he had left the chili in the pot on the stove for the entire three days! It was a safe guess the chili was the source of Charles's attack.

Charles had let his chili sit on the stove for three days.

Since Charles had reheated the chili each night he probably killed off any live microbes. But any toxins that had been made by the bacteria might remain. Charles's first symptom was vomiting and it started only six hours after eating. These clues strongly indicated that Charles's disease was caused by eating bacterial toxins.

My number one suspect was the bacteria *Staphylococcus aureus*. These bacteria are commonly found on our skin and in our noses, so it is easy for them to get into food. Given time they multiply and make very dangerous toxins. They kill our cells by poking holes in them.

SUSPECT: STAPHYLOCOCCUS AUREUS

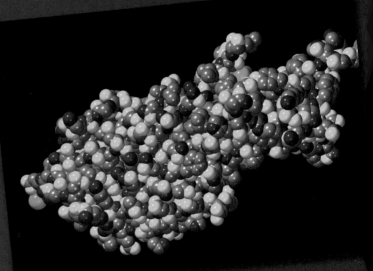

Toxin made by Staphylococcus aureus

Test One — **Was *S. aureus* in Charles's Chili?**

I went back to Charles's house and found the dirty chili pot still in the sink. I took a sample of chili and spread it on Mannitol Salt Agar (MSA). Mannitol is a sugar that *S. aureus* loves. After it eats the mannitol it leaves behind an acid. The acid turns a red dye in the agar to yellow.

Result: Charles's chili turned the MSA agar yellow. The chili I sampled had live *S. aureus* in it. But had Charles eaten *S. aureus* toxins?

① ② ③

V Charles's chili was put on the bottom of the agar plate. Turning the MSA yellow indicates it is *S. aureus*.

Test Two

Were *S. aureus* toxins in the chili?

To help health crime investigators catch this gangster bacteria, companies have developed quick tests for detecting *S. aureus* toxins. I used one of these quick tests on Charles's chili. The test used antibodies made against *S. aureus* toxins. If toxins are present then a color reaction occurs.

Result: The test turned color. This meant that Charles's chili contained *S. aureus* toxins.

The Verdict

Staphylococcus aureus was found guilty on all counts of attacking Charles.

CONVICTED GERM
Staphylococcus aureus

The Case of the Undercooked Burger

Justice

S. aureus poisoning is a horrible illness to experience and there is no cure. Antibiotics don't help because the victim ate toxins and not live bacteria. Because Charles was eighty-five years old, it was possible this attack could have killed him. I kept him in the hospital where he was given lots of fluids to prevent dehydration. Charles was a tough cookie and his immune system was able to triumph over the toxins.

This is Agent Annie Biotica signing off. Stay safe out there.

You Solve the Case

CASE #1

Health investigators are often confronted with attacks on people's digestive systems. Bacterial outlaws use two methods of attack.

Method 1. A person eats live bacteria. The live bacteria set up home inside the victim and begin damaging cells. These bacteria may also produce toxins inside the body.

Method 2. Live bacteria grow on food and fill it with toxins. A person eats the food containing toxins.

For each of the examples below, choose which method of attack (1 or 2) you think has happened.

Example 1: A family spent the day Christmas shopping. When they got home they were exhausted! They decided to order pizza instead of cooking dinner themselves. They were really hungry and ordered a lot of pizza. After eating everyone was so sleepy they went straight to bed. The leftover pizza sat on the kitchen counter. There was so much it sat there for two days until

The Case of the Undercooked Burger

it was all eaten. On the night of the second day everyone in the family was sick.

 Which method do you suspect?

 What bacterium do you suspect?

 How do you think this attack occurred?

Example 2: A young man was in a restaurant and ordered a hamburger. He ordered the burger to be cooked well done. When he got his food he noticed the inside of the burger was very pink and not even hot. He felt uncomfortable sending the burger back so he just ate around the edges. Three days later he was very sick.

Which method of attack do you suspect?

What bacterium do you suspect?

Should the man have eaten a burger with a pink cool center or should he have sent it back to be cooked more?

Example 3: A mother was sick with the flu. Her children decided to make dinner to help out. They took a package of chicken out of the freezer and defrosted it in the microwave. They used a cutting board and sharp knife to cut up the chicken. While the chicken was cooking, they used the cutting board to cut up lettuce and vegetables for a salad. Five days later the family was sick.

Which method of attack do you suspect?

What bacteria do you suspect?

How do you think this attack occurred?

You Solve the Case

A young couple decided to take a trip to a poor country where people do not have running water to wash their hands and have to use outhouses to go to the bathroom.

One day they decided to explore. They rented a jeep and drove up into the mountains. They saw many small villages. For lunch, they ate sandwiches they had brought along with them. After a long day they started back but they got lost. It was very late when they finally stopped at a shack and asked for directions to town. They accepted food from the helpful couple who lived there.

Two weeks later these were their symptoms:

 Nausea

Vomiting

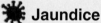 Dark urine that looked like cola

Jaundice

What two symptoms seem to be very important in this case? What criminal do you suspect attacked this young couple? Is this microbe a bacterium, virus, or worm? What could they have done to protect themselves?

You Solve the Case: The Answers

CASE #1 Food Poisoning

Example 1:

Which method do you suspect?
   Method #2

What bacterium do you suspect?
   Staphylococcus aureus

How do you think this attack occurred?
   S. aureus lives on our skin and in our noses. For two days family members exposed the pizza to this bacterium. In two days the bacteria had time to make enough toxin to make the family sick.

Example 2:

Which method of attack do you suspect?
   Method #1

What bacterium do you suspect?
   E. coli O157:H7

Should the young man have eaten a burger with a pink cool center or should he have sent it back to be cooked more?
   He should have sent it back to the kitchen to be fully cooked. Pink and cool centers in ground beef mean that bacteria can still be alive.

Example 3:

Which method of attack do you suspect?
Method #1

What bacteria do you suspect?
Campylobacter jejuni or *Salmonella*

How do you think this attack occurred?
The raw chicken juice on the cutting board contained live bacteria that were transferred to the salad.

CASE #2 Hepatitis A

What two symptoms seem to be very important in this case?
The dark cola-colored urine and jaundice

What criminal do you suspect attacked this young couple?
Hepatitis A

Is this microbe a bacterium, virus, or worm?
A virus

What could they have done to protect themselves?
Before going to the remote country, they could have gotten vaccinated against hepatitis A.

agar: A gelatin substance high in sugar. It gives bacteria a place to grow and food to eat.

agar plate: A petri dish containing agar.

antibiotics: Medicines that inhibit the growth of bacteria.

antibodies: Y-shaped proteins made by the body that help fight off invaders.

anus: The opening in the body where the wastes from digested food are expelled.

bile: A substance made by the liver that helps us digest fatty foods.

colon: The largest part of the large intestine.

DNA: A material inside cells that contains genes.

enzyme: A protein that performs a chemical reaction.

esophagus: The tube that leads from the throat to the stomach.

feces: What is left after all the useful things are removed from our digested food; also called stool.

gall bladder: A small sac that holds and concentrates the liquid bile made in the liver.

gastrointestinal (GI) tract: The long connection of digestive system organs that reaches from the mouth to the anus.

genes: Sections of DNA that code for specific traits, such as eye color.

Gram stain: A chemical test that identifies bacteria as being from one of two groups.

hemolytic uremic syndrome (HUS): A disease caused by *E. coli* O157:H7 in which there is severe kidney damage.

infection: Disease caused by live microbes entering the body.

intoxication: The release of poisonous toxins inside the body.

jaundice: A condition that causes the skin and the whites of the eyes to look yellow.

Glossary

large intestine: Part of GI tract. It lies below the small intestine. This is where water and salt is absorbed into the bloodstream.

larvae: A specific stage in the life cycle of worms and other living things.

Mannitol Salt Agar: A special agar for growing *Staphylococcus aureus*.

normal flora: Bacteria that live in and on our bodies without causing disease.

pancreas: A gland that secretes enzymes into the small intestine that help digest our food.

petri dish: Small plastic dish with a lid. Used for agar plates.

pharynx: A medical term for the throat.

polymerase: The enzyme that copies DNA in the PCR test.

polymerase chain reaction (PCR): A laboratory test that copies the DNA inside a microbe.

rectum: A sac that holds the feces/stool before it is expelled from the body.

small intestine: Part of the GI tract. It lies above the large intestine. This is where most of the nutrients are absorbed out of the digested food into the bloodstream.

Sorbitol MacConkey Agar: A special medium for growing *E. coli* O157:H7.

stool: What is left after all the useful things are removed from our digested food. Also called *feces*.

toxins: Poisons that are produced by microbes.

trachea: The tube that leads from the throat to the lungs.

vaccine: Usually a shot. It gives a person a harmless version of a microbe so that the immune system can begin working on ways to protect itself.

Further Reading

Hayhurst, Chris. *E. coli: Epidemics, Deadly Diseases Throughout History*. New York: Rosen Publishing Group, 2003.

Hoffmann, Gretchen. *Digestive System: The Amazing Human Body*. Tarrytown, N.Y.: Marshall Cavendish Children's Books, 2008.

Horn, Lyle W. *Hepatitis: Deadly Diseases & Epidemics*. New York: Chelsea House Publications, 2005.

Purdie, Kate. *Personal Hygiene: Being Healthy, Feeling Great*. New York: PowerKids Press, 2010.

Sheen, Barbara. *Food Poisoning*. San Diego: Lucent, 2004.

Internet Addresses

Centers for Disease Control and Prevention (CDC). "Campylobacter: General Information."
<http://www.cdc.gov/nczved/divisions/dfbmd/diseases/campylobacter/>

Centers for Disease Control and Prevention (CDC). "FoodNet — Foodborne Diseases Active Surveillance Network."
<http://www.cdc.gov/foodnet/>

U.S. Food and Drug Administration (FDA). "Bad Bug Book: *Staphylococcus aureus*."
<http://www.fda.gov/Food/FoodSafety/FoodborneIllness/FoodborneIllnessFoodbornePathogensNaturalToxins/BadBugBook/ucm070015.htm>

Index

A
agar, 11, 29, 30, 35
    Sorbitol MacConkey Agar, 11
    Mannitol Salt Agar (MSA), 35
antibiotics, 13, 29, 31, 37
antibodies, 23-24
anus, 6
Ascaris lumbricoides, 16, 18

C
Campylobacter jejuni (C. jejuni), 28, 29, 30, 31, 44

D
digestive system, 6, 9, 18, 27, 38
DNA, 12

E
enzymes, 6
Escherichia coli (E. coli), 9-10, 11, 12, 13, 43
espophagus, 6

F
Food and Drug Administration (FDA), 25

G
gastrointestinal (GI) tract, 6
Gram stain, 30

H
hemolytic uremic syndrome (HUS), 13
hepatitis, 22
    hepatitis A virus (HAV), 22, 23-24, 25, 44

I
intestines, 19
    large intestine, 6, 19
    small intestine, 6

J
jaundice, 21, 44

K
kidney, 13

L
large intestine, 6, 19
larvae, 16
liver, 21, 22

M
microbe, 33-34
mouth, 6

N
normal flora, 6

P
pharynx, 6
polymerase chain reaction (PCR) test, 12

S
saliva, 6
Salmonella, 28, 29, 44
small intestine, 6
Staphylococcus aureus (S. aureus), 34, 35, 36, 37, 43
stomach, 6, 15, 17

T
toxins, 6, 10, 13, 34, 35, 36, 37, 38, 43

X
X-rays, 17